The Chosen Path

Tahirih of Persia and Her Search for God

Hussein Ahdieh

Hillary Chapman

THE CHOSEN PATH : TAHIRIH OF PERSIA AND HER SEARCH FOR GOD

ISBN 978-1-923266-25-4 (softcover)
ISBN 978-1-923266-26-1 (ePub)
Second edition, 2025

Distributed by
Bahá'í Distribution Services
173 Mona Vale Rd, Ingleside, NSW, 2101
bds@bahai.org.au
www.bahaibooks.com.au

Body text typeset in 12/19pt Minion Pro
Title text typeset in Monsterrat and Minion 3

Bahá'í
Publications
Australia

Dedicated to junior youth everywhere who strive for the betterment of the world.

The authors would especially like to thank Linda Ahdieh Grant, Tatiana Jordan, and Robert Hanevold for their valuable assistance, and Ivan Lloyd and Simina Rahmatian for their artwork.

Tablet from the Bab concerning the station of Tahirih.

The Bab refers to Tahirih as a proof of God and as *the pure* and *the truthful one*.

CONTENTS

Introduction

By Thomas Grant — Junior Youth from Atlanta

In 1817 a little girl was born who would change the world. Later in her life, she would be called Tahirih, which means *The Pure One* in Arabic. This name was given to her by the Blessed Beauty and the Promised One of all ages, Baha'u'llah. Tahirih was one of the eighteen *Letters of the Living*—the first to recognize the Bab.

The Bab means *The Gate* in Persian. He was the Trumpet Blast announcing Baha'u'llah's Revelation. God sends humanity Divine Messengers to teach mankind how to develop spiritual qualities and contribute to the advancement of society. These messengers are like a new springtime for the world. These Manifestations have come by the names of Abraham, Krishna, Zoroaster, Moses, Buddha, Jesus Christ, Muhammad and now the Bab and Baha'u'llah.

But when messengers come with a new message for a new day, governments and religious leaders of the time are afraid of losing their power and attack the new religion and its Manifestation with all their might. It was the same with the Bab and Baha'u'llah. The religious leaders and the government of Persia (now Iran) were afraid of the new age and teachings the Bab and Baha'u'llah brought. So, they used the full extent of their power to extinguish the teachings of the Twin Manifestations. The Bab and Baha'u'llah suffered every day of their lives. Their followers were tortured and killed because they would not recant their faith.

The Bab Himself was also martyred in the city of Tabriz by a firing squad of seven hundred and fifty guns in a public square. His last words before the guns fired at Him and His young companion were:

> *Had you believed in Me, O Wayward generation, every one of you would have followed the example of this youth, who stood in rank above most of you, and willingly would have sacrificed himself in My path. The day will come when you will have recognized Me; that day I shall have ceased to be with you.*

The Bab's body was shattered that day in Tabriz and after forty years of exile, Baha'u'llah passed away peacefully many years later, but to the present, Their Spirits live on. Today there are followers of The Bab and Baha'u'llah all over the world known as Bahá'ís. The Bahá'í Faith is currently the most widespread religion in the world after Christianity.

In 1844, six years before the Bab's martyrdom, when Tahirih was twenty-seven years old, she recognized the Bab in a dream. In this dream, she saw Him praying devoutly to God. Tahirih was confirmed of His Station when she read some Writings revealed by the Bab and recognized that they were the same words that she had heard the Bab recite in her dream. Her brother-in-law also met and recognized the Bab. He gave the Bab a letter from Tahirih in which she declared that she was ready to accept the Bab's truth and teachings. The Bab then named her as one of his Letters of the Living.

Some years later during a conference of Babis (followers of the Bab) in the town of Badasht, Tahirih entered the meeting without the traditional veil which women were required to wear. Tahirih proclaimed that it was a new day. Those present were stunned and afraid of this act by Tahirih and the message she was announcing; that men and women are created equal and that the Bab's Teachings represented a New Day in human history.

By reading the story of Tahirih, junior youth and youth will be inspired to follow in her footsteps and contribute to the betterment of society and the advancement of civilization. Even though Tahirih's environment during her time was quite different from junior youth and youth today, there are still valuable lessons that one can find in Tahirih's story to help us in our day to day lives. Society sees junior youth as being self-absorbed, unresponsive, problematic and lost in the transition between an adult and a child. But the Baha'i teachings explain that this time in someone's life is vital and can shape their future. It is a time where one's spiritual understanding is the clearest and a time that can be used to serve the world.

Tahirih was persecuted by many people, including her own family, who tried to shake her of her belief. Even when her father-in-law and husband attempted to kill her, she still stayed strong in her faith and continued to spread the Words of God. Tahirih became a famous Persian poet and wrote many poems that talked about the teachings of God and her spiritual journey. Tahirih would teach thousands of people about the Babi Faith and its teachings of how all people were created equal. People would draw to her like a spiritual magnet and their lives would be changed forever.

One day when Tahirih was under house arrest at the mayor's house in the city of Tehran, the mayor's wife came to see her. She saw Tahirih beautifully dressed as if she was ready to meet her Beloved. Tahirih told the mayor's wife that when she was killed, she would like to be thrown into a pit and covered with earth and stones. Tahirih then prayed and fasted. After sunset, soldiers came to the mayor's house to take Tahirih away. She came out dressed in her finest clothes, as if she was going to an event with great importance. The soldiers brought her to a garden outside the city and strangled her with a silk scarf. She was thrown into a pit and covered with earth and stones. Before she was killed Tahirih announced:

You can kill me as soon as you like, but you cannot stop the emancipation of women.

Tahirih's story is an example for everyone—young and old—of how nothing can shake one's beliefs and a story of how one person changed the world.

Prologue

Do you have dreams? What if you had a dream that was telling you something important? Would you believe it? What if everyone else disagreed with what you believed? This is what happened to the young lady in this story.

She had studied the holy books of the past and had come to understand on her own how God was truly working in the world. She believed God was speaking again, this time through a young merchant who claimed that he was the Messenger of God. But very, very few people agreed with her. Most of her family members did not and several of them were even very angry with her. This young woman, though, had confidence in her own thoughts. She used the intelligence God had given her and the education her family had provided her.

When she tried to speak out about these new ideas, she faced another huge challenge: she was a woman. Only men were allowed to speak and teach in public. Still, she persisted. She spoke in public from behind a curtain when men were present. Everywhere she went, she challenged powerful men to debates. She even stood up to the King and his ministers.

What do you think happened to her? Do you think she succeeded?

Chapter 1

Family

Tahirih loved to walk freely through the large rooms of her family's house. Her favorite room was the library because it was filled with books. She loved to read. She was talented and eager to learn. She would grow up to become a great writer and one of the leaders of a new religion. But this would not be easy. She would have to struggle and persevere. Persia was still a traditional society. Women had to follow strict rules which governed their lives. Men were the leaders in society. Only they could be public figures and have a life outside of the home. Women's lives were spent within the family and the home. If a woman needed to go outside to the market, for example, she had to be covered in a *chador*, a large cloth that was usually black and covered her head and body. Her face had to be hidden behind a veil, which was a piece of thin material. Wearing some form of veil was an ancient tradition in this part of the world that continues to this day. Covering a woman's face was meant to preserve her honor. No man was allowed to see her face except the men in her family and her husband. This was especially true for women of noble birth. But these veils were also used to keep women separate and under the control of men. In the house, women had their own private area. The women could relax there, take off their chadors and veils, and speak freely. Men represented the house to the outside world. Only they could act as a host when a male visitor came over. The guest would be received in a special room which had the best rugs and furnishings. The women could only come in and greet the visitor when a man of the family was present.

Fortunately for Tahirih, her father wanted his daughters to be educated. Tahirih attended the girls' section of the school which he had founded. Girls and boys were educated separately and were not allowed to mix in school. Most girls in Persia never got anything more than a basic education if anything at all. Girls learned from their mothers what they needed to know for life. Much of this learning had to do with their future responsibilities in the home as wives and mothers. Girls who came from privileged families would be able to study for more years. Tahirih was from one such family. Her relatives all supported her education. Several of her female relatives were well-educated. If her mother and aunt had been men, they would have been considered as knowledgeable as the most learned of mullas; the title *mulla* meant *priest*, someone who could lead the prayers in the mosque.

Tahirih studied Persian literature and poetry with her mother. Persians had been writing great literature for more than 2,500 years. Rumi, Ferdowsi, and Hafez were three of the most famous Persian poets. There was a lot for Tahirih to read! The men in her family taught her the Qur'an, religious law, Islamic traditions, and various branches of philosophy, the study of knowledge. The Qur'an is the Holy Book of Islam and contains 114 chapters of different lengths, some are quite long while others are short. Tahirih was able to memorize the entire Qur'an at an early age, an accomplishment only the most able students could achieve. Tahirih learned a great deal about the religion of Islam and its rich, centuries-old traditions. It began over a thousand years before she was born, when God chose Muhammad to be His Messenger.

The Prophet Muhammad came from a humble background. He worked as a merchant leading camel caravans between towns. He taught that everyone should worship the one God and perform five duties: to say that there was only one God and Muhammad was His Messenger, to pray five times a day, to give to the poor, to fast once a year for forty days, and to make a pilgrimage to Mecca, the city near to where God first spoke to Muhammad. Those to whom Muhammad gave these Teachings spoke Arabic. The Arabic word for *God* is *Allah*. The words God spoke to Muhammad were written down. They were compiled into a book called the Qur'an, an Arabic word meaning *the Recitation*. There are also many stories about Muhammad and the important things which he said and did which are called the Traditions, or *hadiths*. Islam became the religion of many different cultures and nations so new laws were developed based on the Qur'an by great thinkers who wrote books of Islamic Law and philosophy.

Tahirih was so bright that she ended up being a teacher for her sisters as well. Her brother said later that she was by far the most intelligent and able of the children in the family:

We were all, her brothers and cousins, fearful to speak in her presence, so much did her knowledge intimidate us, and if we hazarded to put forward an opinion on a point of doctrine that was in dispute, she would prove to us where we were going wrong in a manner so clear, precise and magisterial that we were thrown into confusion and withdrew. [1]

Tahirih was the eldest of the seven daughters of her father Mulla Salih, who also had eight sons. He was able to have so many children because he was permitted by law to have more than one wife. The Qur'an allowed this because many women and children had been left without protection when their men were killed in battle during the days of the Prophet Muhammad. Since there weren't enough men for women, Muhammad allowed a man to take another woman as his wife which protected her and her orphaned children. A Muslim could marry up to four wives—men in that part of the world married more in those days—only if he could treat them all fairly. If he could not, he would have to limit himself to one.

Tahirih's father, like her mother, was highly educated. He had been able to receive the title of *mujtahid* because he was a man. Women were not allowed to be mujtahids. A mujtahid was a religious judge. This was a highly respected position in Persia. To achieve this position, a man had to study for many years. People came to them when they had serious disputes with each other. The judges would hear their cases and render verdicts on them. So their decisions could really affect people's lives. Mujtahids could also become wealthy: people paid them to hear their cases, students paid to study with them, and villagers paid them rent to use land they owned.

Tahirih's father and her two uncles, the eldest Mulla Taqi, and the youngest, Mulla Ali, were all mujtahids. The eldest uncle, Mulla Taqi, was greedy for power and influence. He had married one of the daughters of the king so he could become close to him. In Qazvin, he had gotten rich by entering into business deals that were sometimes shady, by pocketing the proceeds from sales of land that no longer had owners, and by charging for his services as a judge even for matters for which payment was not usually required. Though he had become one of the richest clerics in the kingdom this way, [2] he was not well-liked because of these practices.

Mullah Salih did not seek power. Instead, he was interested in developing his school which attracted hundreds of students. The youngest brother, Mullah Ali, taught at this school and was interested in mystical philosophy. Mysticism is the belief that one can be united with God through meditation and contemplation. Ali could be an ascetic, meaning very strict with himself about his spiritual practices such as prayer and study, to the point where he was rumored to chain himself to a wall so he could stay awake and study. [3]

Tahirih showed so much talent that her father wished she had been born a boy so that she could have been a mujtahid and his successor. These men would play very important roles in her life: one would try to destroy her while others would introduce her to new, forbidden knowledge.

Tahirih Studying with Her Sister and Mother at Their Home in Qazvin.
Painting by Simina Rahmatian.

Chapter 2

Marriage

When Tahirih was a teenager, her family decided she would be married to her cousin, Mulla Muhammad, the son of her uncle Taqi. In those days, parents arranged the marriages of their children. Young people did not go out on dates together, hold hands, kiss, or give each other presents. This was considered highly inappropriate. A boy and a girl only really got to know each other after they were married. Though people did love one another, the needs of the family were considered much more important than a person's romantic feelings. What was important was that the bride or groom come from a *good* family—one with a good reputation and which was known to have good morals and possess some wealth and land. Parents tried to find the best match for their child. They hoped that with a good match, their own family's social and economic situation would improve. If parents were poor, it was much harder to make a good match for marriage. The parents of a girl had to pay a dowry—money or property which a bride brought into a marriage—and the smaller of a dowry the family could give the bride for her marriage, the less other families would want their sons to marry her. The dowry was meant as a form of security for the bride as she went into her new marriage but, usually, the husband simply took it for his and his own family's use.

When a child was born, many special prayers were offered. Camphor, a white substance found in oils, might be burned, and sometimes a note with a quotation from the Qur'an used as a talisman—a special object used to bring good luck—might be pinned to the baby's clothing. These and other traditions were done to protect the child from evil spirits and harm. Back in those days, there were no vaccinations because these had not been discovered yet. Babies and young children died of all kinds of illnesses and diseases for which we have medicines today—measles, flus, mumps, and many others. A significant percentage of young children died. Childbirth was dangerous for the mothers as well because they could catch infections from which they died.

The child was named on a special day on which the men of the family gathered with the local mulla and decided on a name. Then the mulla went to see the new mother. Before he entered her room, all the clothing related to women had to be removed, and the mother fully covered. The baby was placed in the mulla's arms, and he recited the chosen name several times and prayed. Once the men left, the women could relax and enjoy themselves by singing, dancing, and playing games.

Families preferred boys because they were much more

privileged in the society; female children were loved as well but not valued as much and sometimes even seen as a burden, such as in the case of the dowry. If a married couple had a baby girl, her life was already mapped out. Very rarely did a little girl have the opportunity to learn even basic reading, writing, and religion. [4] Most of her learning happened in the home by observing and assisting older women who taught them the home skills they would need to be someone's wife. By the time a girl was a teenager, she was considered ready to be married.

Tahirih was blessed because her father and mother both wanted her to be well-educated and were able to provide her with an excellent education. But they also followed the custom of marriage and arranged to have their daughter married to her cousin. Tahirih would go on to have three children with her husband, but they would not have a happy marriage. Tahirih chose a different path than other girls—not the one expected of her by her husband, her father, or traditions and customs. She chose the path towards God.

Chapter 3

Karbila

Tahirih and her husband Mulla Muhammad moved to the holy city of Karbila so that he could continue his studies to become a mujtahid. They joined a caravan and travelled west by road from their city of Qazvin to Karbila. In those days, people travelled in large groups called caravans because there were many dangers on the road, such as bandits who might rob them of any coins, jewels, or other precious items.

Tahirih and her caravan passed under the snowy peaks of the Zagros Mountains which separated the Kingdom of Persia from the Turkish Ottoman Empire. Ottomans were Turkish people who ran an empire that included many of today's countries in the Middle East, such as Turkey, Iraq, Syria, and Israel. Tahirih and her caravan came out of the mountains and down into the flat and hot Mesopotamian plain where Karbila sat between the Euphrates River to the east and the lake of salt to the west.

Karbila was a holy city for Muslims, especially for the Shi'a, one of the two major branches of Islam. After the death of the Prophet

Muhammad, the religion of Islam gradually split into two major
branches: Shi'a and Sunni. The Shi'a followed the authority of holy
men, *Imams*, whom they believed were guided by God and were
descendants of the Prophet Muhammad. Sunnis followed the
authority of the caliph, the political ruler.

Imam Husayn was the third Imam, a divinely-guided holy man
who spoke out against rulers whom he believed were unjust. This
cost him his life. At the Battle of Karbila, in 680 CE, troops sent by
the caliph massacred Husayn and seventy of his companions. His
death is still commemorated every year by Shi'a Muslims who go
out into the street on that day and cry and wail and beat themselves
in memory of his suffering. A magnificent golden-domed mosque
was built over his grave. Karbila became a thriving city. Countless
numbers of Muslims had come there over the centuries to pray at
his grave. Many stayed there because they wanted to be buried near
him, believing this would help their souls in the afterlife.

The young couple spent most of the next thirteen years in
Karbila. Tahirih gave birth to two sons, Ibrahim and Isma'il, and
a daughter, Zaynab. Her life was unfolding in a typical way for a
young woman of her social class. Tahirih, though, was not typical.
She liked to do something that would lead her to dangerous
knowledge: she liked to read books. Powerful men in her family
and throughout the kingdom were going to oppose her. But many
women and men were also going to follow her, hungry for this
dangerous knowledge.

Tahirih with Her Own Young Children in Karbila.
Painting by Simina Rahmatian.

Chapter 4

Shaykhism

Tahirih and her family moved back home to Qazvin after her husband completed his studies. It was there, in her cousin's library, that Tahirih first encountered the dangerous knowledge: Shaykhism, a new way of thinking about the Qur'an and Islam.

Shaykhism was founded by Shaykh Ahmad al-Ahsa'i, an Islamic philosopher who also studied astronomy, medicine, mathematics, and music. He taught that to truly understand the Qur'an, a person had to look at the deeper meaning of its words. When most clerics read the Holy Book, they only used the *literal*, or every day, usual meaning of words. They did not have a *mystical*, or spiritual, understanding. [5] Shaykh Ahmad believed that certain passages in the Qur'an *had* to be read mystically to understand their true meaning: that God was going to send a Promised One soon who would save Islam.

He did not like what he saw in religion. Clerics had become corrupt and narrow-minded, unable to understand the real meaning of the Qur'an, and were not teaching people true religion but only what served their own self-interests. He began to meditate for long periods of time. He had powerful dreams of the Prophet Muhammad and the Imams. [6]

Shaykh Ahmad travelled, taught, and wrote constantly, attracting many students to him. He wrote about one-hundred and thirty-two books and essays, answering many questions that were put to him. The ideas he taught included: God was transcendent— beyond the comprehension of human beings. Human beings were limited to this world so they could not know God in His Essence, meaning as He truly was. Humans were created, but God had not been created. He was Self-Sufficient. Human beings could only know God through His attributes as they were manifested in this world: wisdom, loving-kindness, generosity … but these attributes were according to the understanding of human beings and were not the Essence of God. Because they were dependent, and God was independent, human beings could not come to know God through their own efforts, so God sent Prophets to guide them towards God. Prophets expressed God's Will to human beings in ways they could understand.

Human reason and religion should agree. Shaykh Ahmad interpreted certain verses of the Qur'an mystically because their literal meaning did not make sense—they were not reasonable. One example was the widespread belief among Muslims that after death, the human body would be recomposed and come alive again—the dead would be physically resurrected. Shaykh Ahmad taught that the *body* that continued was the soul, not the physical body. He did

not interpret the Day of Judgment according to tradition as the day
when the world would end, and everyone would be judged. Instead,
he believed that day would be when the Promised One of Islam
would appear. This would be the beginning of a new time. People
would be judged by whether they recognized God's Manifestation
in His new form. Shaykh Ahmad taught that this time was coming
soon, so he wanted to prepare his students to recognize Him. [7]

Shaykh Ahmad's teachings created great excitement among
his students. When he passed away, his students were guided
by his successor, Siyyid Kazim. Tahirih read the writings of the
Shaykhis and became more and more convinced that they were
true. Soon she was a devoted follower of the Shaykhi teaching. But
this became a major problem. Her husband, Mulla Muhammad,
and his father, Mulla Taqi, were totally opposed to the Shaykhi
teachings. Taqi, who was ambitious and thirsted for greater and
greater wealth, sided with the more traditional view of Islam and
thought that by opposing Shaykh Ahmad, he could increase his
own prestige among traditional Muslims who were the majority.
He went so far as to issue an edict calling Shaykh Ahmad an
infidel[8]—an unbeliever—which was shocking because Ahmad was
a respected Islamic scholar even though he had unusual views. [9]

In this debate, her father, Mulla Salih, acted as a peacekeeper.
Her younger uncle, Mullah Ali, came to agree with the Shaykhi
teachings. Her marriage now became much more strained. She
was willing to follow her beliefs whether her husband approved of
them or not, and he was not willing to allow this or to change his

own ideas. Tahirih had to move out of their home and back into her father's house. She decided to go and find Siyyid Kazim in the city of Karbila. She left on her journey with her sister, daughter, and others. Her husband kept their two sons with him. She remained forever separated from her sons who grew up to be important Shi'a clerics. But when her sons were mentioned in future history books about important Shi'a figures of this period, they were listed as sons of *al-Qurat ul-Ayn*, meaning Tahirih, showing the great respect in which she came to be held.

Chapter 5

The Promised One

A young Shaykhi cleric was making his way towards the gate of the city of Shiraz, unaware that he was about to walk out onto the stage of world history. He had come to Shiraz because he believed that the Promised One of Islam had appeared in the world and that he had to go out and seek him. After his teacher's passing, this young cleric, Mulla Husayn, had secluded himself in one of the oldest mosques in the Islamic world, because his teacher had told him to purify himself before beginning his quest. So he prayed and fasted for forty days and forty nights, and when he was ready, he arose and went out on his search.

Mulla Husayn's prayers led him to Shiraz. To enter Shiraz in those days, one had to pass through a gate, a beautiful large structure where people met up with one another. Mulla Husayn arrived in Shiraz on a hot and sunny afternoon. He sent his companions ahead to find a place to stay for the night. Then a young man walked up to him and greeted him with great warmth. He had a gentle manner and refined appearance. He wore a green

turban which indicated that he was a *siyyid*, a descendant of the
Prophet Muhammad. His name was Siyyid Ali Muhammad. Mulla
Husayn thought to himself that this young man must be a fellow
Shaykhi who had come out to greet him.

Evening was approaching. Siyyid Ali Muhammad invited him to
his home for dinner. He told Mulla Husayn not to worry about his
companions who had gone ahead:

*Commit them to the care of God; He will surely protect and
watch over them.*

Mulla Husayn followed the young man to his house. They
walked through streets lined by walls on both sides—houses in the
Middle East faced inward and did not have windows looking out
onto the street. They arrived at a wooden door. A servant opened
it, and the two stepped into a refreshing little courtyard which had
a pool of water and an orange tree. They climbed up the stairs to
the upper room. After praying, Siyyid Ali Muhammad asked Mulla
Husayn what he was seeking. Mulla Husayn answered that his
teacher had told him that the Promised One of the age had come
and that he must go out and find him. He listed several of the signs
of the Promised One. Siyyid Ali Muhammad asserted:

Behold, all these signs are manifest in Me.

Mulla Husayn was shocked by this answer. He quickly tried
to come up with arguments as to why this was impossible. He
showed the young siyyid a theological essay he had written. Siyyid

Ali Muhammad quickly looked over Mulla Husayn's complex points about the Promised One in the Qur'an. He then revealed the deeper meanings that Mulla Husayn had not understood. The young man spoke with great power and authority, not at all like someone his age. Out of the blue, the young siyyid then offered to write a commentary on the Qur'anic chapter about Joseph, the son of Jacob. Mulla Husayn was stunned by this offer because his teacher had told him that only the Promised One would be capable of doing this.

The words flowed quickly from the young siyyid:

The overpowering effect of the manner in which He wrote was heightened by the gentle intonation of His voice which accompanied His writing. Not for one moment did He interrupt the flow of the verses which streamed from His pen ... I sat enraptured by the magic of His voice and the sweeping force of His revelation.'

Mulla Husayn knew that he had found the object of his quest: the Promised One of God, the Renewer of the world!

Siyyid Ali Muhammad proclaimed to him:

O thou who art the first to believe in Me! Verily I say, I am the Báb, the Gate of God, and thou art the Bábu'l-Báb, the gate of that Gate. Eighteen souls must, in the beginning, spontaneously and of their own accord, accept Me, and recognize the truth of My Revelation. Unwarned and uninvited, each of these must seek independently to find Me ... [10]

Mulla Husayn remembered how the revelation hit him:

*… I felt possessed of such courage and power that were the
world, all its peoples and its potentates, to rise against me,
I would, alone and undaunted, withstand their onslaught.
The universe seemed but a handful of dust in my grasp. I
seemed to be the voice of Gabriel personified, calling unto
all mankind: 'Awake, for, lo! the morning Light has broken.
Arise, for His Cause is made manifest. The portal of His
grace is open wide; enter therein, O peoples of the world! For
He Who is your Promised One is come!'*[11]

At dawn, on 23 May 1844, Mulla Husayn stepped back out
into the street, a man who was changed by 'a sense of gladness
and strength.' Over that summer of 1844, one seeker after another
found the Bab. Among them was the extraordinary woman who
became one of his foremost disciples: Tahirih of Qazvin.

Chapter 6

Tahirih's Dream

By early 1844 when the Bab declared Himself, Tahirih was living in the city of Karbila which was holy to Shi'a Muslims because the third Imam, Husayn, was buried there. The city was also a center for the study of the Islamic religion. Tahirih's father, Mulla Salih, hoped that by allowing his daughter to go on this journey to the holy city, she would lose interest in the radical Shaykhi ideas. Her husband felt humiliated that he had such a strong-headed wife who would choose different beliefs than his own and act so independently. Her uncle actively preached and taught against the Shaykhis.

Tahirih made the journey to Karbila with her sister and brother-in-law in the hope of studying with Siyyid Kazim, the leader of the Shaykhis. Unfortunately, Siyyid Kazim passed away before Tahirih arrived in Karbila. [12] His widow was greatly impressed by her and invited her to stay in her home. The widow's love for Tahirih aroused the interest of other women. [13] Soon Tahirih was giving classes in Siyyid Kazim's widow's home which attracted both men and women who wanted to hear this extraordinary woman.[14] Her reputation as a spiritual visionary spread throughout the friendship networks of the women who attended her classes.

Women, though, were not supposed to be teachers of religion. That was a man's job. Still, there were many men interested in what she was teaching. When they came, she spoke from behind a curtain because in this society it would have been inappropriate for her to show her face and speak in public in front of men.

Siyyid Kazim told the Shaykhis to go and find the Promised One of the Age. But after the death of Siyyid Kazim, many Shaykhis didn't do this. It was more comfortable for them just to study and teach. But Tahirih knew that she must actively go out and seek the Promised One. She really believed He was here. Several other Shaykhis also set out on the same quest as Mulla Husayn. Tahirih's brother-in-law, Mulla Muhammad Ali Qazvini was one of them. She gave him a letter she had written for the Promised One. She instructed her brother-in-law to give it to the Promised One if he found Him[15] and:

Say to Him, from me, the effulgence of Thy face flashed forth, and the rays of Thy visage rose high. Then speak the word, 'Am I not your Lord?' and 'Thou art, Thou art!' we will all reply.[16]

In this poem, she wrote joyfully about the arrival of the new day:

Wake up, sleeper! Your lover's come for you! Rouse yourself, brush those cobwebs from your hair ...[17]

Then one night in the summer of 1844, Tahirih had a dream[18] in which she saw a young siyyid dressed in black with a green turban on his head, and his hands raised up in prayer.[19] He spoke words that stayed with her even after she had woken up. Around the time she had this dream, her brother-in-law found the goal of his quest: the Bab, the Promised One. He gave Him Tahirih's letter. The Bab read it and immediately declared her to be one of his apostles. The Bab gave her the title of *Letter of the Living*.[20] The Letters of the Living were the Bab's disciples who were to carry his message out to the people. Tahirih was the only one of them who was a woman. They were the Letters because they were formed by the Primal Point, the Bab—like a Pen which forms letters on a page.

Tahirih became confirmed in her faith when she read a copy of the text revealed by the Bab on the night of His declaration to Mulla Husayn.[21] Tahirih recognized immediately that these words were the same as those she had heard in her dream. She was now certain she had found the object of her spiritual search—the Promised One of the age foretold by her Shaykhi spiritual teachers.[22]

Tahirih Teaching Women and Girls.
Painting by Simina Rahmatian.

Chapter 7

Tahirih, the Pure One

Eighteen souls came on their own through dreams and study and personal encounters with the Bab to believe that He was the Promised One. In October, 1844, the Bab decided to go to Mecca, where the Prophet Muhammad had born and the holiest city in Islam, to proclaim that he was the Promised One of Islam. He crossed the sea from Persia to Arabia. In Mecca, he stood up next to the Kaba'a, the holiest shrine in Islam, and proclaimed His message but his words fell on deaf ears. He then prayed intensely at the tomb of Muhammad, the Messenger of God whose time He was fulfilling.

In Karbila, Tahirih saw it as her duty to teach others about the Bab's message and to remove any doubts about His claims. She wrote a poem about how those with insight must try to help others develop their inner vision such that they can see God in whatever form He makes Himself manifest. [23]

He's come! He's here to tear our veils away
He's here! He's come to show us God today ... [24]

She translated the Bab's Writings from Arabic into Persian so
that her countrymen could read them. She knew both languages
well.

Tahirih taught the Bab's message boldly and publicly. She wrote
long letters to all the leading clerics of Karbila explaining the true
station of the Bab. She told them to stop trying to prevent the
spread of His teachings. This was astonishing because she was a
woman attempting to teach prominent men who viewed women
as inferior beings without souls. Tahirih also needed to educate the
Babis. Most Babis did not fully understand the claims of the Bab.
They believed that the Bab would purify Islam so that the religion
would return to its former glory. But they were sure there would be
no *new* Revelations from God because they had been taught that
Muhammad was the last Manifestation of God.

Tahirih, though, had studied the Bab's Writings carefully, and
had come to understand that in every age God would send a new
Manifestation of God and that the Bab was the bringer of the
new Divine Revelation—not just the reformer of Islam. For most
Muslim clerics and Shaykhis, and many Babis, this was much too
radical a claim. Still, she continued to speak out and teach. She
faced her opponents courageously and taught what she believed
to be true. From 1844 to 1847, many people—men and women—
came to learn from her. A group of students developed around her.

They spread the ideas she taught. She had high standards for her group of students: they had to keep good habits around her such as not smoking or swearing.

Tahirih lost an important protector in early 1846, when Siyyid Kazim's widow passed away. [25] Attacks on Tahirih mounted, so she moved to the nearby town of Kazimayn. [26] Once she moved there, she was free to teach and, again, she drew large crowds. [27] She challenged the prominent mullahs to a public debate, but they declined probably because they were intimidated by her brilliance. [28] Instead, conservative clerics spread rumors about her to try to turn the Babis of Kazimayn against her. [29]

Spreading rumors can really harm a person. Even if the rumor is not true, when people hear it about another, they can't get it out of their heads, and it gives them a bad impression of that person. Rumors also harm the spiritual life of those who spread them because they are hurting someone else. The rumors spread about Tahirih had their intended effect because Persia was a deeply conservative society, so such rumors shocked people. The Babis of Kazimayn decided to write to the Bab directly about Tahirih's teaching and activities. [30] In those days, the mail took a long time to reach its destination because it had to go by horse. By the time the Bab's reply arrived, Tahirih had already left Kazimayn. [31] His answer was read to a gathering of Babis. The Bab supported Tahirih's understanding of his teachings. He called her the *Pure One* which is what *Tahirih* means, and He even regarded her as the leader of the Babis of that whole region.

Through all of these intense attacks, Tahirih's love for the Bab remained constant. She had a deep desire for reunion with God which she expresses in this, her most famous poem:

If ever I should behold you
face to face,
eye to eye, I would be bold to recount
My heart's plaint
point by point,
Verse by verse.

Like Saba the east wind,
I have searched everywhere
for your countenance
from house to house,
door to door,
alley to alley,
from quarter to quarter.

Bereft of your visage,
my two eyes have wept
such bloody tears,
Tigris after Tigris,
stream upon stream,
spring after spring,
brook upon brook.

Your bloom-like mouth,
your face enveloped
with ambergris hair,

blossom to blossom,
flower to flower,
tulip to tulip,
fragrance to fragrance;

Your perfect brow,
your eyes, your beauty spot
have preyed on the bird of my heart,
sense to sense
and heart to heart,
feeling to feeling
and mood to mood.

My desperate heart
has knitted your love
to the very fabric of my being,
string by string,
thread by thread,
warp by warp,
and woof by woof.

Táhirih has searched
every layer of her heart
but found only you there,
sheet by sheet,
fold by fold,
cover by cover
over and over again. [32]

Tahirih with Ladies Drinking Tea.
Painting by Ivan Lloyd.

Chapter 8

Tahirih Unloosed

The false rumors about Tahirih had reached her father back in Qazvin. She wrote imploringly to him:

> I plead with you! This humblest of people is your daughter. You know her, and she has been brought up and educated under your supervision. If she had, or has, a worldly love, that could not have remained a secret to you. If you want to inquire into her affairs, God who holds the scale and is the remover of veils would testify for her. [33]

Tahirih's mission was to teach about the coming of the Promised One, but this always met with great opposition. She even challenged her father on this:

> Dear Father! So many times when I visit the holy shrine of the Imam, may peace be upon him, in the flood of my tears I pity you and pray for you that perhaps you may be saved …

If you fail to recognize the cause, there will be no benefit for you in all your acts of devotion. [34]

Back in Karbila, opposition to Tahirih grew fiercer. She was placed under house arrest. [35] Tahirih defended herself by saying that all she wanted was an open debate with religious authorities so that the truth of the teachings could be established. [36] But no one took her up on her offer, possibly fearing that her great knowledge would prove the claims about the Bab to be true. Finally, she left Karbila for Baghdad. On the way out, angry residents—stoked by clerics—threw stones at her. [37]

Tahirih arrived in Baghdad sometime in early 1847 and immediately began to teach publicly in the house that was provided to her. [38] She had translated important works by the Bab and used all of these for her classes. [39] Her influence continued to spread. The chief judge of Baghdad summoned Tahirih to an interview. He found her to be innocent of heresy, [40] but he wanted to be sure of this. So, he sent her to be interviewed by Shaykh Alusi, a cleric who had previously tried and banished another of the Bab's Letters of the Living. Alusi was also very impressed by Tahirih. Not only did he not find her to be a heretic, but he was interested in her claims. Later in his life, Shaykh Alusi remembered his interview with Tahirih:

Verily, I saw in her such a degree of merit and accomplishment as I rarely saw in men. She was a wise and decent woman who was unique in virtue and chastity … there is no doubt about her knowledge. [41]

Tahirih also taught Persian Jews about the Bab. Jews had been living in Persia for over four thousand years, since before the time of Islam. A Jewish doctor, Hakim Masih, who was accompanying the King of Persia on a trip, attended a gathering of Muslim clerics in Baghdad. They were debating with a woman who spoke from behind a curtain. This was Tahirih. Her arguments were so logical and expressed with such force and clarity that he became a believer. Since he had never heard of the Bab, he thought that this woman was herself the Promised One. He was able to hear Tahirih speak three more times before he had to resume his journey with the Shah. When he returned to Tihran, he treated a Babi prisoner who taught him about Tahirih and the Bab. Through Masih's subsequent teaching, many Jews became Babis.

The Ottoman Turkish authorities decided that her teaching, combined with her popularity, constituted a threat and would make tensions between the Sunni Muslims, who were Arabs and Turks, and the Shi'a Muslims, who were mostly Persian, much worse. Since Tahirih was Persian, they ordered her to be sent back to Qazvin in Persia. A representative of her family arrived in Baghdad to bring her back. He observed in a letter to Tahirih's father that

> the entire nobility and the 'ulama of Baghdad greatly respect her and confer on her highest praises. [42]

Tahirih left Baghdad around March 1847, accompanied by Ottoman officials, about thirty of her followers, and her female companions. The journey through the mountains took about three months. All along the way, she taught fearlessly about the appearance of a new revelation from God and met with both resistance and acceptance. [43] In the village of Karand, hundreds of excited people swore allegiance to Tahirih. The hearts of these rural people were open and not jaded like those of city people. They said they were willing to serve as her personal army which she, of course, declined. In these villages of Western Iran, many people followed a religion called Ahl-e Haqq, which taught that God made Himself known through successive manifestations so her message of a new manifestation of God may have appealed to them. [44]

Tahirih and her group arrived in Kirmanshah, on the Western border of Persia. [45] Many of the people in this city also followed the Ahl-e Haqq religion. Tahirih spent forty days there during which she met with the governor, his wife, and other prominent citizens. [46] Her presence and teaching excited the people. She challenged the religious leaders to a public debate[47] which worried the chief mujtahid. He asked the governor to have her and her followers thrown out of town. The governor replied that she had offered to have a public debate and to have both parties pray to God asking Him to show which party was in the wrong. [48] The chief mujtahid rejected both of these options, most likely because they were too risky with a person as talented as Tahirih.

An enemy of the governor then organized a physical attack on Tahirih and her companions. The companions were beaten, and their goods were stolen. [49] She and a few of her closest companions were put into a coach and sent out of the city into the desert without any provisions. [50] Tahirih wrote to the governor describing how they had been treated. He found out that the clerics were behind all of this and ordered the mayor to return all their belongings. [51]

Next, Tahirih stopped in the important city of Hamadan. With the help of the prominent women of the city, she challenged the religious leaders to a debate. She wanted them to follow certain rules: the debate must be on prophecies about the Promised One and the participants must refrain from bad language and smoking. The smoking of water pipes, even opium, was common at religious debates, but she insisted on certain rules of purity just as the Bab had. *Purity* in religion is the idea that your mind, body, and habits are all clean—that your clothes are not soiled, that your mind is not filled with evil thoughts, that you don't curse when speaking, and that you don't smoke or take drugs or alcohol. Cleanliness is an attribute of God.

In the debate, she explained the basic Babi doctrines that divine revelation was ongoing and progressive, that the Bab was giving a new teaching for a new age, and that the Babis were its recipients. The clerics chose as their spokesperson a great Sufi mystic. Sufis believed that the source of human suffering was disconnection from the Creator and that all human beings had the potential to be re-united with Him. While the Sufi mystic treated her and her ideas respectfully, another mujtahid verbally attacked her. He was rebuked by the governor who then closed the debate. [52]

Soon Tahirih's teaching in Hamadan was bringing more Jewish

people into the new Faith. Jews had lived in Persia for thousands
of years. People of the various religions in Persia, though, did
not mix socially and rarely inter-married. A person almost never
converted to another religion as this would have created great
problems with the family and community who would have seen
this as abandoning tradition. In April 1847, Mulla Lazar, son of the
leading rabbi of Hamadan, hosted Tahirih in his home. His father
became concerned that her presence in a Jewish home might bring
on anti-Jewish violence. [53] So the daughter of the late King offered
to host Tahirih. [54] News of Tahirih's teaching in Hamadan travelled
through the networks of highly educated women. For her safety,
Tahirih was moved to a village owned by the Turkish noblewomen
of Hamadan, and then she left for Qazvin with her relatives. [55]

Chapter 9

Murder

After three years away, Tahirih arrived back in her hometown of Qazvin in July 1847. Her family was deeply divided by the Bab's claims, and she was returning to Qazvin as one of the acknowledged leaders of the Babi Faith. [56] The Writings of the Bab had arrived there before Tahirih's return. Some people enthusiastically became Babis. Others rejected the new teachings, such as Tahirih's uncle, Mulla Taqi, who stepped up his attacks on the Babis.

Her family held a council on her first night back. Her father told her that if she had been born a man and declared herself to be the Bab, he would have believed her, but he couldn't understand her devotion to this *Shirazi lad* as he referred to the Bab. [57] He wanted more than anything to keep peace in the family. She responded to her father that she had come to her faith through thoughtful study and prayer. She assured him that she knew what she was doing. Her

uncle Taqi flew into a fury when she said this. He cursed the Bab
and then struck her. She warned him that she saw his mouth filled
with blood. [58]

Tahirih moved to her brother's house where she held classes
for women. [59] She was also in constant correspondence with the
Bab who was imprisoned in the remote stone fortress of Mahku.
Her estranged husband sent her a message telling her to return to
their home. She replied that he had rejected the religion of God.
She could have changed his unbelief into belief, she said, if he had
stood by her, but he hadn't. Now, she was casting him out of her
life forever and divorcing him. This angered her husband and his
father, Mulla Taqi. They set about to undermine her and the Babis
in every way. [60]

Babis were insulted in public and humiliated by having their
turbans unwound and used to drag them around. Rumors were
spread about Tahirih's family. Her uncle Taqi was especially angry
about this because this was his family as well and all of this affected
their reputation. He became even more aggressive in his attacks
on Babis. [61] Her father did not believe these rumors and denied
them. Still, they ashamed him. Public reputation in Persian society
was very important. If a person had been insulted or slandered,
they could not simply let it go. It had to be made right and the
reputation restored. It would have been intolerable for a person
or family—especially a prominent one—to allow their name
to be besmirched. But Tahirih's father could never escape the
humiliation. Because of this, he had to leave Qazvin years later for
Iraq where he died. [62]

In his anger, Mulla Taqi denounced the new teachings from
the pulpit in the mosque. He insulted the founder of Shaykhism,
Shaykh Ahmad, still a respected figure.[63] This angered a sincere
young Shaykhi so much that he resolved to kill Taqi. The young
man entered the mosque in the evening. At sunrise, he crept
out from his hiding place and stabbed Taqi while he performed
his dawn prayers.[64] He fled up to the roof leaving Taqi's bloody
body on the mosque floor. People rushed into the mosque.[65] The
authorities went out searching for Babis to arrest.[66] The attacker
was bothered by this, so he gave himself up to the governor. He was
brought to the death bed of Taqi who identified him.[67]

The shocking murder of a high-ranking cleric like Mulla
Taqi gave the enemies of Tahirih the perfect pretext with which
to destroy the Babi community of Qazvin. Her husband, Mulla
Muhammad, and his associates rounded up prominent Babis.
Homes of Babis were raided and ransacked.[68] Women were also
attacked.[69] A mob forced Tahirih and her maid out of her father's
house. The governor interrogated Tahirih who defended herself
eloquently. The governor then threatened to brand them when
news arrived that the killer had turned himself in.[70]

There was no evidence that Tahirih had played any role in
this crime, so she was released into house arrest in her father's
home. Her husband and one of her cousins plotted to poison her
food.[71] Tahirih did not eat the household food in case it had
been poisoned.[72] No one was allowed to visit her except a faithful
friend[73] who made excuses like washing Tahirih's clothes, so she

could bring her news and food. Though Tahirih's innocence made
it impossible for her husband to punish her, he was able to destroy
several of the leading Babis of Qazvin. These were the first public
executions of the followers of the new faith in Persia and included
the first Babi—one of Tahirih's Arab followers—to be killed on
Persian soil. [74] The killings were carried out with great cruelty by
mobs in the streets who were incited by clerics.

Tahirih challenged the unjust actions of her estranged husband,
Mulla Muhammad, who had now succeeded his father as the
leading cleric of Qazvin. She sent him a message from the Qur'an
which stated that only unbelievers rejected God's light when it
appeared. She wrote that if she was not delivered from him in nine
days, this would be a sign that she had been wrong.

> 'Fain would they put out God's light with their mouths; but
> God only desireth to perfect His light, albeit the infidels
> abhor it.' (Qur'an, 9:33). If my Cause be the Cause of Truth,
> if the Lord whom I worship be none other than the one
> true God, He will, ere nine days have elapsed, deliver me
> from the yoke of your tyranny. Should He fail to achieve my
> deliverance, you are free to act as you desire. You will have
> irrevocably established the falsity of my belief. [75]

Mulla Muhammad ignored the message.

Mirza Husayn Ali, the prominent Babi leader, decided that
the time had come to rescue Tahirih from the violence in Qazvin
unleashed by her husband who sought revenge on her. The wife of

one of his trusted friends[76] disguised herself as a beggar woman and took a sealed letter to the house where Tahirih was being kept prisoner.[77] Soon, Tahirih was secretly taken away to another location. When her captors realized she had escaped, they searched for her everywhere. Tahirih and two companions were brought to the city wall, near a gate where three fast horses were waiting for them. They rode ninety miles to Tihran through the cold October night, taking a back road to avoid detection.[78] They stopped at a shrine a couple of miles to the west of the capital.[79] Tahirih and her group were able to rest in the garden, while a messenger went into town to let Mirza Husayn Ali know they had arrived.[80]

Tahirih Escaping from Qazvin.
Painting by Ivan Lloyd.

Chapter 10

The Trial of the Bab

The Bab's influence spread throughout Persia. Thousands of people were eager to hear that God was speaking again. Even if they weren't sure of what the Bab was claiming, they were drawn to the excitement of a spiritual renewal. What the Bab was claiming, though, really mattered. If he was claiming to be an inspired teacher of the Qur'an, that was okay. There had been many distinguished scholars and mystics whom people had followed. But if he was claiming to be the bringer of a new Revelation from God like Muhammad, that was heresy. Heresy means to teach ideas that are against official religious doctrine and, in that time, it was a crime that could be punished by death.

Because of the Bab's growing popularity, the authorities decided that he had to be put in a prison far away from anyone. They chose the fortress of Mahku, a stone fort located in the far northwest of Persia on the border with Russia. Its four large towers stood up on a rock mountain looking down over a valley. A lone path connected the gate of the fort to the town at the foot of the mountain. The people of this area were Kurds who followed the Sunni form of Islam. When the local farmers went out to their fields in the morning, they often stopped to look up at the stone fortress hoping to receive a blessing from the holy man being kept within it.

Gradually the Bab's spirituality changed the warden and the guards. The warden had a vision of the Bab walking outside the walls of the fortress. After this, he allowed visitors to come in and see the Bab. [81] His influence spread. The Bab transformed Mahku from a remote prison fortress into a center of spiritual attraction. A bitterly cold winter took hold of this region. From his dark and cold stone room, [82] the Bab began to reveal his Holy book, the Bayan (the *Utterance*). This was the new Book of God, and He was a new Manifestation of God. The Prime Minister read reports about the Bab's growing influence on the hearts of the local people. So, in April 1848, the Prime Minister had the Bab moved south to the prison fortress of Chihriq located in an even more remote Kurdish region. The rules there were supposed to be even stricter. The Bab referred to Chihriq as the *Grievous Mountain*. But the isolation could not stop the spread of the Bab's spiritual power. Soon the officer in charge of the prison fortress allowed people to come and meet this Holy figure. One man walked all the way from India to meet the Bab after seeing Him in a dream. [83]

Back in Tehran, the authorities decided that it was time to put the Bab on trial. The most prominent clerics and the crown prince of Persia gathered in Tabriz, the main city of the region where the Bab was being held a prisoner. News of His coming spread. All along the road to Tabriz, people flocked to see the Bab. Stories were told of miracles that occurred in His Presence.[84] The clerics wanted to know exactly who the Bab was claiming to be. The Bab entered and without being asked, sat in the seat of honor. When questioned about his claim, He answered:

> *I am, I am, I am, the Promised One! I am the One whose name you have for a thousand years invoked, at whose mention you have risen, whose advent you have longed to witness, and the hour of whose Revelation you have prayed God to hasten.*[85]

This was an astounding thing for a man to claim. How could this young man from Shiraz be the Promised One of Islam? He was not a learned man, after all, like the assembled clerics. He had no signs of power, like a King had, no army or riches. He was a prisoner in a remote area of the Kingdom. The Bab's claim angered several of the clerics. They wanted to embarrass this youth who was making such a preposterous claim. They wanted Him to prove that He was the Promised One. The Bab answered that His own word was the

> *… most convincing truth of the Mission of the Prophet of God.*[86]

A cleric asked Him to describe the trial in the style of the language of the Qur'an. If the Bab was the Promised One of God,

He should be able to speak in the same language of Revelation as Muhammad had done in the Holy Book. But the Bab spoke an unconventional form of Arabic. As he started to answer the request, a cleric cut him off by saying He had made some grammar mistakes. At that point the Bab uttered the Qur'anic verse:

Far be the glory of thy Lord, the Lord of all greatness, from what they impute to Him, and peace be upon His Apostles![87]

He got up and walked out of the trial. The clerics then argued among themselves. The trial ended in confusion.

A religious decree was issued condemning the Bab to death. It was not carried out, though, because the authorities were afraid that he would become even more popular as a martyr. Instead, he was whipped like a common criminal. But news of the trial's proceedings spread throughout Tabriz, and the reputation of the Bab grew. The authorities took him away and isolated him back in the mountain fortress of Chihriq. [88]

Meanwhile, Tahirih had been rescued from the violence in Qazvin. Because of her uncle's murder, his son, who was her former husband, began violent persecutions against the Babis. Mirza Husayn Ali had her taken away by night and brought her to Tehran. Tahirih sensed that he had very great spiritual capacity, and he was admired and respected by everyone and came from a distinguished family. Protected by Mirza Husayn Ali, Tahirih spent time in hiding in his home in Tihran. Her voice, though, was becoming stronger and even more unafraid. One evening in Tihran, Vahid, who had given up his position as one of Persia's highest-ranking clerics by becoming a Babi, was visiting the home of Mirza Husayn Ali. Tahirih listened to Vahid speaking about signs and prophecies in the Qur'an. Suddenly, she interrupted Vahid:

> *Let deeds, not words, testify to thy faith, if thou art a man of true learning. Cease idly repeating the traditions of the past, for the day of service, of steadfast action, is come. Now is the time to show forth the true signs of God, to rend asunder the veils of idle fancy, to promote the Word of God, and to sacrifice ourselves in His path. Let deeds, not words, be our adorning.* [89]

Tahirih and Vahid.
Painting by Simina Rahmatian.

Chapter 11

Badasht

Mirza Husayn Ali organized a gathering of Babis at the village of Badasht in the province of Khorasan. Tahirih and her personal servant rode through Tihran's northern gate. They had to be careful because the city's gatekeepers were on the alert for any woman without a pass. Seven or eight miles outside of the city, they came to a large house in the middle of an orchard at the foot of the mountains whose owner had abandoned it. Its elderly caretaker was there and agreed to look after the two women as they prepared for the long journey east. For this kind of long ride overland, people had to make sure they had enough food, money, and protection. A person couldn't just ride off and hope to make the long journey safely as there were no police and the only rest areas were in large towns which had caravanserai, a type of inn. Most importantly, travelers could bring their horses and camels into them and have them fed. There were also rooms—usually quite dirty—for people to sleep in, but there were no beds. Tahirih and her group took the main east-west highway across Persia. With no trees, dust from all the other travelers riding donkeys, horses, and camels filled the air. [90]

They rode until they reached a town that was at the juncture of the roads that went east and north to the sea. Tahirih's destination—the village of Badasht—was to the South. This area had been a resort for the nobility because it had flowing water and trees. There were several small gardens with a large open area in the middle where the Babis could gather to meet. [91] Mirza Husayn Ali rented three gardens. One was for himself, another for Quddus, and a third for Tahirih; other believers pitched their tents near them. [92] Each garden had a large tent with mats and carpets. There was a stream which ran through the great open field, the fruit trees were in bloom, and great mountains could be seen on the horizon. [93]

Eighty-one Babis gathered at Badasht in the beginning of the summer of 1848. [94] To prepare for this gathering, the Bab and Mirza Husayn Ali had corresponded frequently. [95] The Bab had revealed His Holy Book, the Bayan, just the winter before so the Babis did not know it well. In those days, you had to have a physical copy of a book to read it and things travelled much more slowly than today. The main purpose of this gathering was to determine the true nature of the Bab's Revelation. The Babis did not all have the same understanding of the Claims of the Bab. Was he announcing a new Revelation or was he the promised reformer of Islam? If this was a *new* Revelation, *what* were its teachings and *who* were its leaders?

Some believed that the Bab was the fulfillment of Islam while others thought that He was a complete break with the past—a new Messenger from God like Muhammad. Tahirih believed that Bab had brought a new revelation. Islamic Law was now replaced with a new law and a new teaching. For many Babis this was very radical—maybe too much. All their relatives and ancestors going as far back in time as they could remember had been raised according to the Law of the Qur'an. It was unimaginable—and even frightening—to think that this had all changed.

One day, Mirza Husayn Ali was ill in His tent. Quddus and other believers came to meet with Him. They were speaking with Him when Tahirih entered their gathering. Looking up at her they were shocked because she was not wearing the traditional veil without her veil. She proclaimed to the gathering that:

> *The Trumpet is sounding! The great Trump is blown!*
> *The universal Advent is now proclaimed!*[96]

These were words from the Qur'an and the Book of Isaiah. On the new Day of God, a trumpet blast would be heard and would announce it. In ancient towns a trumpet would sound when there were important announcements or news that everyone had to hear. She, Tahirih, a woman, was that trumpet blast. [97]

Shoghi Effendi later wrote about this event:

A little over four years had elapsed since the birth of the Báb's Revelation when the trumpet-blast announcing the formal extinction of the old, and the inauguration of the new Dispensation was sounded … The trumpeter was a lone woman, the noblest of her sex in that Dispensation, whom even some of her co-religionists pronounced a heretic. The call she sounded was the death-knell of the twelve hundred year old law of Islám. [98]

The Babis were shocked by this. They regarded Tahirih as being the same as Fatimih, Muhammad's daughter, whom they considered to be holy. This was a conservative society, so to look upon a woman's face was considered scandalous. To look upon the face of a holy woman was blasphemous. When they saw Tahirih unveiled and proclaiming the New Day some of the Babis there may have remembered the Islamic tradition in which Fatimih appears unveiled on the Day of Judgement. They may have realized that the time had come. [99] Many of those who witnessed this were shocked; one Babi even cut his own throat as a gesture of atonement for having looked on the face of such a holy person. [100]

Tahirih was shattering the boundaries of appropriate female behavior. She was driven by powerful spiritual forces which she believed had been released into the world because of the Bab's revelation. Being a woman was not a limitation for her, but a source of power. In this poem, she celebrates her own strength as a woman:

Just let the wind untie my perfumed hair, my net would
capture every wild gazelle.

Just let me paint my flashing eyes with black, and I would
turn the day as dark as hell.

Yearning, each dawn, to see my dazzling face, the heaven
lifts its golden looking-glass … [101]

The Babis all looked to Mirza Husayn Ali for guidance. He told
them to read this Surih of the Inevitable from the Qur'an:

When the Day that must come shall have come suddenly …
Day that shall abase! Day that shall exalt … [102]

That Day had come. Even in all the commotion, Tahirih
appeared radiant and peaceful. She spoke about this new time
using Qur'anic language. She declared herself to be the word of this
revelation:

I am the word that the Qa'im will utter, the word that shall
put to flight the chiefs and nobles of the earth. [103]

And she encouraged those assembled to celebrate this day:

This day is the day of festivity and universal rejoicing, the
day on which the fetters of the past are burst asunder. Let
those who have shared in this great achievement arise and
embrace each other. [104]

Tahirih's actions divided the Babis. Some now doubted the truth of the Bab, and a few even left the Faith. [105] It was Mirza Husayn Ali's wisdom which held the Babis together. He guided them to a new understanding of the Bab's revelation. Though no written record survives of Badasht, the Babis came to understand that the Bab's revelation was a new Revelation. Now, every day at Badasht, another law of Islam was abolished, [106] followed by a vigorous discussion among the Babis. Mirza Husayn Ali steered the course of these events. [107] He was able to create unity among the Babis. On each of the twenty-two days at Badasht, He revealed one tablet which was chanted aloud. He gave new names to individual Babis. He was now *Baha*, meaning *Glory* or *Glorious One*; there was no objection to him having this title because of the respect in which he was held by the other Babis. Tahirih was now known by this name which the Bab had called her and meant the *Pure One*; prior to that she had been known by other names, such as *Qurratu'l-Ayn*, meaning the *solace of the eyes*. [108] In tablets to his followers, the Bab used the new names they had been given at Badasht. [109]

After Badasht, the Babis went back out into the world greatly changed. They were leaping into the unknown. What if you began a new life in which everything you believed had changed?

Tahirih at Badasht.

Painting by Ivan Lloyd.

Chapter 12

Taken Prisoner

After Badasht, Tahirih, Quddus, Jinab-i-Baha, and others travelled north along a river through a high mountain pass into a valley which went all the way to the Caspian Sea. Tahirih composed and chanted poems aloud in praise of the new day. The sound of her voice echoed in the valley.[110] Tahirih spent the next year and a half under the protection of Jinab-i-Baha in the province of Mazindaran where his family owned land and homes in the district of Nur. The province of Mazindaran was full of green valleys and flowers. The Alborz Mountains rose up in the southern part of the province and dropped dramatically into the coastal plain of the Caspian Sea. This was a beautiful region of Persia.

Jinab-i-Baha's father, Mirza Buzurg, owned several villages and homes in Nur, where he had built a large mansion in the village of Takur. The villagers had seen Jinab-i-Baha grow up there as a boy and respected the whole family. Takur sat in a dramatic setting.

Mountain peaks soared north of the village and the Nur River valley opened to the south, the river flowing through a canyon with a sheer rock cliff. Mirza Buzurg's large house dominated the village of simple stone and brick homes with rocky lanes meandering between them. The arch above the two-story mansion had an inscription:

> *When thou enterest the sacred abode of the Beloved, say: 'I am at thy command. This is the home of Love; enter with reverence. This is holy ground; remove thy shoes when thou enterest here.'*[111]

From his ancestral village, Jinab-i-Baha guided the affairs of the dynamic new religion. In the summer of 1848, Mulla Husayn led a group of Babis across Persia to proclaim the message of the Bab.[112] By the time he reached Mazindaran, he had over three-hundred people with him.[113] As they neared the town of Barfurush, a large and angry crowd confronted them believing that the Babis would destroy Islam. Soldiers treacherously attacked the Babis as they were leaving. Mulla Husayn led the Babis to a local shrine dedicated to a holy man named Shaykh Tabarsi. There, the Babis built a simple fort and set up camp.[114] While they were building the fort, the Babis were frequently attacked by local people. Quddus joined them several days later. This brought great joy to the Babis. He was greatly revered by them; Mulla Husayn even called himself Quddus' *lowly servant*. Then the Babis gathered together to chant the Writings of the Bab.[115]

The leading cleric in the region wrote a letter of alarm to the new King of Persia, Nasir al-din Shah, warning him that there was a rebellion taking place and that troops were needed. Though the Babis were untrained, they were determined and had faith. They were able to repulse the attacks of the professional soldiers. Army reinforcements arrived and surrounded the fort. Despite the overwhelming odds in favor of the army, the standoff continued through that winter of 1848-49. Mulla Husayn led several charges which terrified the soldiers. In one of the charges, he was killed. With inspiration from Quddus, the grieving Babis managed to continue their struggle. The food supplies dwindled. The Babis were hungry and cold. The cannons were constantly firing at them. But they did not give up.

Finally, officials used a trick. They lured the Babis out by swearing an oath on a Qur'an that they were guaranteed their safe passage. People back then took oaths very seriously, especially one made on the Holy Book. Quddus responded faithfully to the oath. The Babis marched out. They were immediately seized and massacred except for a few who were taken as slaves. Quddus was spared only so that he could be brought back to his hometown of Barfurush where he suffered an appallingly cruel martyrdom. A street mob made knife cuts in his body and filled the wounds with lit candles. In his dying moments he asked for forgiveness for his tormentors. [116]

When she heard about the events at Tabarsi, Tahirih wanted to disguise herself as a man and join the others, but Jinab-i-Baha discouraged her from going. [117] Tahirih spent 1849 under his protection living in various towns and villages in Mazindaran. The Prime Minister of Persia considered Tahirih a wanted Babi rebel, and near the year's end, government agents found her in a farmhouse and killed her host on the spot. [118] She was taken back to Tihran as a prisoner to begin the last phase of her life.

Chapter 13

Martyrdom of the Bab

In January 1850, Tahirih was brought to Tihran as a prisoner. This sprawling capital city of over one hundred thousand people lay on a flat plain. The foothills of the Alborz Mountains rose up in the north. Long paths connected it to the villages and countryside. The palace of the king, government buildings, and the major bazaars were built in the foothills north of the city. The wealthy also constructed their mansions with private gardens up in the foothills where the weather was mild and where they were in closer proximity to the royal family. Jinab-i-Baha's father had an estate there named *the abode of the birds*.

The vast majority of people lived in the south part of Tihran. That section of the city was a jumble of small buildings and uneven and mostly unpaved streets and alleys. The poor lived in crowded streets that stunk of animal and human waste. It smelled especially bad during the hot and dusty summer months. Though

Jinab-i-Baha was wealthy, he and his new wife spent much time serving the poor in south Tihran. [119]

Tahirih was soon summoned to an interview with the Prime Minister and the King. [120] The King must have been very impressed by her, because he may have offered to make her one of his wives. She rejected the King's offer. Tahirih was placed under house arrest in the home of the mayor of Tihran. [121] Because of the respect in which she was held, she was allowed to visit certain other homes. [122] The wife of the Mayor became devoted to Tahirih, and many of the aristocratic women of Tihran came over to learn from her. [123]

One of those women was a prominent poet, Shams-i-Jahan, the grand-daughter of a former King of Persia. [124] She arrived at the Mayor's house, stepped into the inner courtyard and crossed over to the building where Tahirih was being held on the second floor. She said a prayer asking God that if Tahirih's teachings were true, she would be allowed to see her. Then a second-floor window opened. Tahirih appeared in it *like a brilliant sun* and called down to her. Overcome with emotion, the princess began to cry. Tahirih smiled. The princess asked her about her imprisonment. Tahirih answered that it was because she proclaimed the truth. The princess understood that this *truth* was the teachings of the young Siyyid from Shiraz. Suddenly, their conversation was cut off by guards. The princess had to leave but longed to continue their talk on these spiritual questions. [125]

Tahirih generated excitement among the prominent women of the capital. One evening, a wedding feast was held in the Mayor's house for his son. Decorations hung everywhere. Singers and musicians were brought in. Princesses and wives of important government officials came dressed in all of their finery. The celebration got under way with music playing and food being served. The women sent a message to the mayor—men and women were separated from one another—asking that he allow Tahirih to come and speak to them. Tahirih entered with great dignity and spoke with such power that the women forgot the wedding. She moved them to tears as she recounted her trials and tribulations and then comforted them with humorous stories. She finished by walking among them chanting her poems. After this night, even the maids and helpers in the home became deeply attached to Tahirih. [126]

But it was around this time that Tahirih would be dealt a blow that would break her heart. The authorities had determined that the time had come to destroy the Babi Faith which was only becoming more and more popular. This undermined the power of the clergy. The Bab may well have known that his own days were coming to an end. He wrote letters of instruction to important disciples, calling on them to carry out specific missions. He sent a locked coffer to his most important disciple, Jinab-i-Baha, which contained letters, seals, pens and pen-cases, and rings. In those days, letters were written in beautiful calligraphy, decorative handwriting that is like drawing letters and was greatly respected among Persians. Pens or brushes were dipped in ink to create the beautiful script. When a letter was finished, it would be closed with wax on which a person pressed their seal to show that it was from them. The Bab wrote in a refined calligraphy. His letters were small and graceful. He wrote one message on a scroll of delicate blue paper which was made up of 500 verses with 360 derivations of the word *Baha* written in the form of a pentacle, a five-pointed star in a circle. [127]

In fact, the authorities had decided that the time had come to execute the Bab. They believed that by killing the person who was the head of the Faith, the Faith would die. The death warrant was signed. On 9 July 1850, the Bab, the young man who had caused a spiritual revolution, was executed by a firing squad in Tabriz along with a young Babi who had begged to ascend with him. The Bab had once described himself this way:

> *I am the Mystic Fane, which the Hand of Omnipotence hath*
> *reared. I am the Lamp which the Finger of God hath lit*
> *within its niche and caused to shine with deathless splendor.*
> *I am the Flame of that supernal Light that glowed upon*
> *Sinai in the gladsome Spot, and lay concealed in the midst of*
> *the Burning Bush.* [128]

Tahirih wrote this poem which shows how she must have felt during this painful period. Here, she returns to a theme often expressed with great power in her poetry—separation from the Beloved:

... Lift me, love, on the wings of my desire
Lift me to you, to safety in your fire

Only take me up, away from this place
Set me down in the place that is no place

Yet keep me close to you, far from strife,
since in this empty world, I have no life. [129]

Soon, the time came when Tahirih would join her Beloved.

Persian Town Square.
Painting by Ivan Lloyd.

Chapter 14

Martyrdom of Tahirih

On 15 August 1852, several Babis attempted to kill the King of
Persia while he was out for a ride. Jinab-i-Baha had warned them in
the strongest terms not to take such an action. Taking revenge was
against the teachings of the Bab. But they did not listen. The men
had pulled the king off his horse and shot at him. The gun was so
poorly made that it malfunctioned. The King was not badly hurt,
but the attack traumatized him. He unleashed a great persecution
of the Babis throughout his kingdom. Jinab-i-Baha was taken on
foot and in chains down to the capital under a broiling sun and past
the shouts and jeers of onlookers on the road. The people of Tihran
were in a frenzy. [130]

The authorities also turned on Tahirih who had been under
house arrest in Tihran. Two important clerics were chosen to
question her. [131] They concluded that her views were heretical, and
they sentenced her to death. [132] One day, the wife of the mayor

came up to her room to see her. The fragrance of perfume filled the
air. Tahirih told her that she was going to meet her beloved—the
time of her martyrdom was coming soon. When that time came,
she wished her body to be placed in the ground and covered over.
The wife of the mayor became filled with anxiety upon hearing this;
she had grown to truly love her guest. Tahirih instructed her not
to allow anyone else into her room because she wanted to fast and
pray now. The wife of the mayor, in fear over the loss of the woman
she loved, went repeatedly up to her room to listen for sounds. She
could hear Tahirih chanting.

Three hours after sunset, soldiers cleared the streets around the
mayor's house. No one must witness them taking Tahirih out. They
were ordered to fire on anyone who approached. At four hours
after sunset, soldiers arrived at the door of the mayor's house and
demanded that Tahirih come with them. The frightened mayor's
wife approached her room trembling. Tahirih emerged dressed
in her finest clothes, veiled and perfumed as if she was going to
an event of the greatest importance. Before going downstairs, she
gave the mayor's wife the key to a chest of her belongings and told
her that these objects were to help her to remember her gladness
at the hour of martyrdom. Tahirih asked that the son of the mayor
accompany her to make sure that the soldiers did not handle her
body and to act as a go-between for her. Downstairs, the soldiers
waited with a horse for the prisoner. A cloak was put over her for a
disguise. They rode through the dark streets until they reached the
Ilkhani garden outside the gate of the city. There, an army officer

and his soldiers were drinking. The son approached the officer who ordered that Tahirih be executed. The son went with two men and gave them her handkerchief to be used for this purpose. Among her last public words, she issued this powerful prediction:

You can kill me as soon as you like, but you cannot stop the emancipation of women. [133]

The men strangled her. Then the mayor's son and several others lowered her body into an empty well and covered it with stones and dirt. Everyone dispersed. [134]

Behind them, they left the body of one of the most extraordinary women in the spiritual and cultural history of Persia. The Baha'i history, *God Passes By*, wrote that she had followed

… the path she chose for herself, and from which she never swerved from the moment of her conversion to the hour of her death. [135]

Back at the mayor's mansion, his wife leaned over the chest containing the few items Tahirih had left behind in this world:

… as I stood beside her chest, wondering what could have induced so great a woman to forsake all the riches and honours with which she had been surrounded and to identify herself with the cause of an obscure youth from Shiraz. What could have been the secret, I thought to myself, of the power that tore her away from her home and kindred, that

sustained her throughout her stormy career, end eventually
carried her to her grave? Could that force, I pondered,
be of God? Could the hand of the Almighty have guided
her destiny and steered her course amidst the perils of her
life?[136]

To Tahirih, however, this death was life itself; separation from
her Beloved was the real death. Her death meant reunion with him.
Martyrdom was the last gift she could give to express her love for
the Bab:

> *I will lay my head in the dust before your face.*
> *My idol, this is the holy law I embrace …*
>
> *No life flows from my soul, my tomb brings no ending.*
> *To be with you is life, and separation death.*
>
> *As I lay dying, your lips moved to speak a word*
> *Of care, and that is the one thing that gives me breath.* [137]

Scene of Tahirih's Martyrdom.

Painting by Ivan Lloyd.

Reflection Questions

Chapter 1:

(1) What does the word persevere mean? Is it good to persevere? Why or why not? Is there something in which you would like to persevere?

(2) What is the Holy Book of Islam?

(3) How was Tahirih's family different from other families in her society?

(4) Is education important? Why or why not? Is it important for both boys and girls to be educated? Why or why not?

Chapter 2:

(5) How did people become married in Tahirih's time? How is that different from today?

(6) What is a dowry? Why were these paid?

Chapter 3:

(7) Who was the Imam Husayn? Why is he important in Islamic history?

(8) Who are the Imams?

(9) Who is the head of the Christian religion? Who is the head of the Baha'i Faith?

Chapter 4:

(10) What is Shaykhism and who was its founder?

(11) What is reason? Give several examples of a person using 'reason'. Can a person have religious beliefs and be reasonable? Why or why not?

(12) How did the men in Tahirih's family react to the Shaykhi teachings?

Chapter 5:

(13) Mullah Husayn was on a search. Whom was he seeking? What does it mean to seek?

(14) What convinced Mullah Husayn that the Bab was the Promised One? What did the Bab tell Mullah Husayn would happen next?

Chapter 6:

(15) What did Tahirih see in her dream? How did she become a follower of the Bab?

(16) What title was she given by the Bab?

(17) Do you believe dreams having meaning? Why or why not?

Chapter 7:

(18) What is a rumor? Why is it harmful to spread them? Can you give an example?

(19) Why is backbiting wrong? What can you do if you hear someone backbiting?

(20) In response to the rumors about Tahirih, how did the Bab describe her?

Chapter 8:

   (21) How can religion divide people? Give examples. How can religion unite people? Give examples. Why does religion sometimes divide people?

   (22) Why were Tahirih's offers of public debate always rejected?

Chapter 9:

   (23) What is persecution? Why is it wrong? For what reasons are some groups of people persecuted? Can you think of examples of famous persecutions?

   (24) How did Tahirih react to the persecutions of the Babis? What would you have done?

Chapter 10:

   (25) How did the Bab's presence at Mah-Ku and Chihriq affect the local people? Why do you think the Bab had this effect?

   (26) What is the Holy Book revealed by the Bab? What is the Holy Book of Islam? Of Christianity? What is a 'Holy Book' and what makes it special compared to other books?

Chapter 11:

   (27) Who organized the Conference at Badasht?

   (28) Why was the Conference of Badasht held?

   (29) What did the Babis decide?

   (30) What is the significance of Tahirih removing her veil?

Chapter 12:

    (31) Why were the Babis under attack at Fort Tabarsi?

    (32) Why was Mullah Husayn leading a group of Babis across the country?

    (33) What does it mean to 'proclaim a message'?

Chapter 13:

    (34) What effect did Tahirih have on the women of Tihran? Why do you think she had this effect?

    (35) Why was the Bab put to death?

    (36) What are several of the phrases Shoghi Effendi uses to describe the Bab?

Chapter 14:

    (37) Does religion allow violence? Have people committed violence in the name of religion? Why? Can you think of examples?

    (38) Was Tahirih frightened of dying? Why or why not?

    (39) What are some words or phrases you would use to describe Tahirih? Why did you choose those?

Endnotes

[1]   Nabil-i-Zarandi, *The Dawn-Breakers: Nabil's Narrative of the Early Days of the Bahá'í Revelation*, trans. Shoghi Effendi (Wilmette, IL: Baha'i Publishing Trust,1932), 84.

[2]   Abbas Amanat, *Resurrection and Renewal, the Making of the Babi Movement in Iran, 1844-1850* (Ithaca, NY: Cornell U. Press, 1989), 318.

[3]   Mírzá Asadu'lláh Fádil-i Mázandarání, *Zuhúr al-Haqq*, Volumes 1–4 (Tihrán, Iran: Bahá'í Publishing Trust, 1973), 306.

[4]   Afsaneh Najmabadi "Education xxv. Women's Education in the Qajar Period." *Encyclopaedia Iranica*, ed. Ehsan Yarshater, accessed October 18, 2013, http://www.iranicaonline.org/articles/education-xxv-womens-education-in-the-qajar-period.

[5]   Vahid Rafati, *The Development of Shaykhi Thought in Shi'i Islam* (PhD diss., UCLA, 1979), 9.

[6]   Ibid., 42.

[7]   Ibid., 106-22.

[8]   Shoghi Effendi, *God Passes By* (Wilmette, IL: Bahá'í Publishing Trust, 1979), 196.

[9]   Moojan Momen, "Usuli, Akhbari, Shaykhi, Babi: The Tribulations of a Qazvin Family." *Iranian Studies* 36, no. 3 (2003): 317–37.

[10]   Nabil-i-Zarandi, *The Dawn-Breakers,* 39-45.

[11]   Ibid., 65.

[12]   'Abdu'l-Baha, *Memorials of the Faithful* (Wilmette, IL: Baha'i publishing Trust, 1971), 192.

[13]   Nabil-i-Zarandi, *The Dawn-Breakers,* 193.

[14]   Mázandarání, *Zuhúr al-Haqq*, 313.

[15]   H. M. Balyuzi, *The Bab* (Oxford: George Ronald, 1973), 26.

[16]   Nabil-i-Zarandi, *The Dawn-Breakers,* 56.

[17]   Amin Banani, and Jascha Kessler, *A Portrait in Poetry*, Ed. Anthony Lee (Los Angeles: Kalimat Press, 2004), 75.

[18]   'Abdu'l-Baha, *Memorials of the Faithful*, 190.

[19]   Ibid., 193.

[20]   Tahirih's brothers-in-law, Mirza Muhammad Ali Qazvini and Mirza Hadi Qazvini, sons of Haji Mirza Abdu'l-Vahhab, her father-in-law/uncle, and Taqi's main rival in Qazvin, were Letters of the Living (Nabíl-i-Zarandi, *The Dawn-Breakers,* 55).

[21]   Balyuzi, *The Bab*, 726-58; the text was the "Ahsanu'l-Qisas" ("The Best of Stories") the commentary on the Surih of Joseph revealed by the Bab ('Abdu'l-Baha, 191).

[22]   'Abdu'l-Baha, *Memorials of the Faithful*, 193.

[23]   John Hatcher and Amrollah Hemmat, *The Poetry of Tahirih* (Oxford: George Ronald, 2002), 40.

[24]   Banani and Kessler, *A Portrait in Poetry*, 51.

[25]   Abbas Amanat, "Qurrat al-'Ayn: The Remover of the Veil," in *Tahirih in History: Perspectives on Qurrat al-'Ayn from East and West*, ed. Sabir Afaqi, (Los Angeles: Kalimat Press, 2004), 149, n. 35.

[26]   Ibid., 118.

[27]   Mazandarání, *Zuhúr al-Haqq*, 252.

[28]   Nosratollah Mohammad Hoseini, *Hadrat-i-Tahirih* (Dundas, Ontario, Canada: Association for Baha'i Studies in Persian, 2000), 200.

[29]   Amanat, "Qurrat al-'Ayn," 124.

[30]   Balyuzi, *The Bab*, 163.

[31]   According to Amanat (*Tahirih in History,* 151, n. 77), the Bab's reply came in mid-1261 AH.

[32]   Hatcher and Hemmat, *The Poetry of Tahirih*, 102-3.

[33]   Amanat, "Qurrat al-'Ayn," 126.

[34]   Ibid.

[35]   Nabil-i-Zarandi, *The Dawn-Breakers*, 278.

[36]   Amanat, "Qurrat al-'Ayn," 125-6, n. 86.

[37]   Root, Martha, *Táhirih the Pure* (Los Angeles: Kalimat Press, 198), 61.

[38]   Balyuzi, *The Bab*, 162.

[39]   Ibid., 163.

[40]   Amanat, "Qurrat al-'Ayn", 127.

[41]   Ibid.

[42]   Ibid.

[43]   Ibid., 130.

[44]   Ibid., 130.

[45]   Root, *Táhirih, the Pure,* 64.

[46]   Amanat, "Qurrat al-'Ayn," 130.

[47]   Ibid.

[48]   Ibid.

[49]   Balyuzi, *The Bab*, 164.

[50] Root, *Táhirih the Pure,* 64.

[51] Ibid.

[52] Mazandaráni, *Zuhúr al-Haqq,* 310.

[53] Mehrdad Amanat, *Jewish Identities in Iran: Resistance and Conversion to Islam and the Baha'i Faith* (I.B. Taurus: NY, NY, 2011), 95.

[54] Ibid., 235, n. 28.

[55] Ibid., 165.

[56] Amanat, "Qurrat al-'Ayn," 133.

[57] Root, *Táhirih the Pure,* 69.

[58] Ibid., 70.

[59] 'Abdu'l-Baha, *Memorials of the Faithful,* 197.

[60] Nabil-i-Zarandi, *The Dawn-Breakers,* 195.

[61] Ibid., 195-6.

[62] Momen, "Usuli, Akhbari, Shaykhi, Babi," 333.

[63] Nabil-i-Zarandi, *The Dawn-Breakers,* 196.

[64] Ibid., 197.

[65] Ibid., 197.

[66] 'Abdu'l-Baha, *Memorials of the Faithful,* 198.

[67] Nabil-i-Zarandi, *The Dawn-Breakers,* 197.

[68] Haji Siyyid Asad'ullah and his son Mihdi's house was ransacked; he was a faithful believer whose daughter was a sister-in-law to Tahirih (Root, *Táhirih the Pure,* 75). Mulla Mushin known as the 'Babi killer', and government agents raided the homes of known Babis (Samandar, "Biography of Tahirih", 54).

[69] Samandar, quoted in Root, *Táhirih the Pure,* 74.

[70] According to Root (*Táhirih the Pure,* 74), Tahirih's maid was about to be branded. They were saved when Tahirih turned in prayer towards Mahku where the Bab was imprisoned.

[71] Hoseini, *Hadrat-i-Tahirih,* 238.

[72] Samandar, quoted in Root, *Táhirih the Pure,* 74-75.

[73] Khatun Jan the eldest daughter of Haji Asad'u'llah (Root, *Táhirih, the Pure,* 75).

[74] Balyuzi, *The Bab,* 166.

[75] Nabil-i-Zarandi, *The Dawn-Breakers,* 203.

[76] Hadi Qazvini, husband of Khatun Jan ('Abdu'l-Baha, *Memorials of the Faithful,* 199). According to Samandar (quoted in Root, *Táhirih the Pure,* 75), Khatun Jan was the eldest daughter of Haji Asadullah, of the Farhadi

family. She was the one who secretly visited Tahirih. This Hadi had left Qazvin before the agitation but was sent back there by Baha'u'llah to rescue Tahirih.

[77]   Nabil-i-Zarandi, *The Dawn-Breakers*, 203.

[78]   Root, *Táhirih the Pure*, 76.

[79]   Ibid.

[80]   According to Samandar (quoted in Root, *Táhirih the Pure*, 58), Tahirih rested while Aqa Hadi went into the city and told Karbala'i Hasan Tajere Qazvini that Tahirih had arrived. Karbala'i Hasan Tajere Qazvini came out to the garden of Imam Zadi where she was staying. Quli didn't know him and hit him but Tahirih told him to stop. She brought fruits out and shared the food with him.

[81]   Nabil-i-Zarandi, *The Dawn-Breakers*, 173-4.

[82]   Ibid., 176.

[83]   Ibid., 219-21.

[84]   Ibid., 226-7.

[85]   Ibid., 229.

[86]   Ibid., 230.

[87]   Ibid., 231.

[88]   Ibid., 232-3.

[89]   'Abdu'l-Baha, *Memorials of the Faithful*, 200.

[90]   David S. Ruhe, *Robe of Light: the Prophetic Years of the Supreme Prophet Baha'u'llah 1917-1852* (Oxford, UK: George Ronald, 1994), 83-4.

[91]   Root, *Táhirih the Pure*, 81.

[92]   'Abdu'l-Baha, *Memorials of the Faithful*, 200.

[93]   Ibid.

[94]   According to Shaykh Abu Turab (quoted in Nabil-i-Zarandi, *The Dawn-Breakers*, 211).

[95]   Shoghi Effendi, *God Passes By*, 31.

[96]   The Qur'an, Surah 74:8 and 6:73 (quoted in 'Abdu'l-Baha, *Memorials of the Faithful*, 201).

[97]   Shoghi Effendi, *God Passes By*, 33-4.

[98]   Ibid.

[99]   Ibid., 32.

[100] According to Shaykh Abu Turab (quoted in Nabil-i-Zarandi, *The Dawn-Breakers*, 213).

[101] Banani and Kessler, *A Portrait in Poetry*, 49.

[102] The Qur'an, Surah 56 (quoted in 'Abdu'l-Baha, *Memorials of the Faithful,* 201).

[103] Nabil-i-Zarandi, *The Dawn-Breakers,* 213.

[104] Ibid., 214.

[105] 'Abdu'l-Baha, *Memorials of the Faithful,* 201.

[106] According to Shaykh Abu Turab (quoted in Nabil-i-Zarandi, *The Dawn-Breakers,* 211).

[107] Shoghi Effendi, *God Passes By,* 31-2.

[108] Hoseini, *Hadrat-i-Tahirih,* 176.

[109] According to Shaykh Abu Turab (quoted in Nabil-i-Zarandi, *The Dawn-Breakers,* 211).

[110] Ruhe, *Robe of Light,* 91.

[111] Ibid., 40-1.

[112] Nabil-i-Zarandi, *The Dawn-Breakers,* 235-7.

[113] Moojan Momen, "The Social Basis of the Babi Upheavals in Iran (1848-1853): A Preliminary Analysis," *International Journal of Middle East Studies* 15, no. 2, (1983): 161.

[114] Nabil-i-Zarandi, *The Dawn-Breakers,* 237-48.

[115] Ibid., 250-7.

[116] Ibid., 259-98.

[117] Root, *Táhirih the Pure,* 88.

[118] Amanat, "Qurrat al-'Ayn," 157, n. 179.

[119] Ruhe, *Robe of Light,* 24, 50-2.

[120] Root, *Táhirih the Pure,* 95-96.

[121] Shoghi Effendi, *God Passes By,* 74.

[122] Ruhe, *Robe of Light* footnote *, 111.

[123] 'Abdu'l-Baha, *Memorials of the Faithful,* 202.

[124] Amanat, "Qurrat al-'Ayn," 143, n. 179.

[125] Jinab-i-Avarih, "The Story of the Princess," *Star of the West* 14, no. 12 (1924): 359-360.

[126] Abdu'l-Baha, *Memorials of the Faithful,* 202.

[127] Shoghi Effendi, *God Passes By,* 69.

[128] The Bab, *Selections from the Writings of the Bab,* (Haifa, Israel: Bahá'í World Centre, 1982), 74.

[129] Banani and Kessler, *A Portrait in Poetry,* 92-93.

[130] Ruhe, *Robe of Light,* 146-7.

[131]   Shoghi Effendi, *God Passes By,* 74.

[132]   Ibid.

[133]   Ibid., 75.

[134]   'Abdu'l-Baha, *Memorials of the Faithful,* 203-204.

[135]   Shoghi Effendi, *God Passes By,* 76-7.

[136]   Nabil-i-Zarandi, *The Dawn-Breakers,* 458-9.

[137]   Banani and Kessler, *A Portrait in Poetry,* 73.

Bibliography

'Abdu'l-Baha. *Memorials of the Faithful*. Wilmette, IL: Baha'i publishing Trust, 1971.

Amanat, Abbas. "Qurrat al-'Ayn: The Remover of the Veil." In *Tahirih in History: Perspectives on Qurrat al-'Ayn from East and West*, edited by Sabir Afaqi, 113–158. Los Angeles: Kalimat Press, 2004.

———. *Resurrection and Renewal, the Making of the Babi Movement in Iran, 1844-1850*. Ithaca, NY: Cornell University Press, 1989.

Amanat, Mehrdad. *Jewish Identities in Iran: Resistance and Conversion to Islam and the Baha'i Faith*. New York, NY: I.B. Taurus, 2011.

Bab, The. *Selections from the Writings of the Bab*. Haifa, Israel: Bahá'í World Centre, 1982.

Balyuzi, H. M. *The Bab*. Oxford: George Ronald, 1973.

Banani, Amin, and Jascha Kessler. *A Portrait in Poetry*. Edited by Anthony Lee. Los Angeles: Kalimat Press, 2004.

Effendi, Shoghi. *God Passes By*. Wilmette, IL: Bahá'í Publishing Trust, 1979.

Hatcher, John, and Amrollah Hemmat. *The Poetry of Tahirih*. Oxford: George Ronald, 2002.

Hoseini, Nosratollah Mohammad. *Hadrat-i-Tahirih*. Dundas, Ontario, Canada: Association for Baha'i Studies in Persian, 2000.

Jinab-i-Avarih. "The Story of the Princess." *Star of the West* 14, no. 12 (1924): 359–360.

Mázandaráni, Mírzá Asadu'lláh Fádil-i. *Zuhúr al-Haqq*, Volumes 1–4. Tihrán, Iran: Bahá'í Publishing Trust, 1973.

Momen, Moojan. "The Social Basis of the Babi Upheavals in Iran (1848- 1853): A Preliminary Analysis." *International Journal of Middle East Studies* 15, no. 2 (1983): 157–183.

———. "Usuli, Akhbari, Shaykhi, Babi: The Tribulations of a Qazvin Family." *Iranian Studies* 36, no. 3 (2003): 317–337.

Nabil-i-Zarandi. *The Dawn-Breakers: Nabil's Narrative of the Early Days of the Bahá'í Revelation*. Translated by Shoghi Effendi. Wilmette, IL: Baha'i Publishing Trust, 1932.

Najmabadi, Afsaneh. "Education xxv. Women's Education in the Qajar Period."
    Encyclopaedia Iranica. Edited by Ehsan Yarshater. Accessed October 18, 2013.
    http://www.iranicaonline.org/articles/education-xxv-womens-education-in-
    the-qajar-period.

Qur'an, The.

Rafati, Vahid. *The Development of Shaykhi Thought in Shi'i Islam*. PhD diss.,
    UCLA, 1979.

Root, Martha. *Tahirih the Pure*. Los Angeles: Kalimat Press, 1982.

Ruhe, David S. *Robe of Light: the Prophetic Years of the Supreme Prophet
    Baha'u'llah 1917-1852*. Oxford, UK: George Ronald, 1994.

Samandar. "Biography of Tahirih." Cited in Martha Root, *Tahirih the Pure*. Los
    Angeles: Kalimat Press, 1982.

Author Biography

Hussein Ahdieh moved to the USA as a teenager to pursue a Master's Degree in European Intellectual History and a Doctorate in Education from the University of Massachusetts. He helped to establish the world-renowned Harlem Preparatory School in New York City and was the Director of Higher Educational Programs at Fordham University.

Hillary Chapman is a writer, songwriter, teacher, and guitarist. He is a fourth generation American Baha'i who is the grandson of Hand of the Cause Leroy loas, who worked closely with Shoghi Effendi and Ruhiyyih Khanum. He holds degrees from Haverford College, the University of Pennsylvania, and a diploma from the University of Paris.

Dr Ahdieh and Mr Chapman are co-authors of:

- *Rúhíyyih Khánum*
- *Awakening: A History of the Bábí and Bahá'í Faiths in Nayríz*
- *A Way Out of No Way: HarlemPrep: Transforming Dropouts into Scholars*
- *'Abdu'l-Bahá in New York*
- *Foreigner: From an Iranian Village to New York City*
- *The Calling: Tahirih of Persia and the women of the Great Awakening*

www.ingramcontent.com/pod-product-compliance
Lightning Source LLC
Chambersburg PA
CBHW072008060426
42446CB00042B/2236